T0005048

POLLUTION

INFO PICS

BY HARRIET BRUNDLE

Gareth Stevens
PUBLISHING

Please visit our website, www.garethstevens.com. For a free color catalog of all our high-quality books, call toll free 1-800-542-2595 or fax 1-877-542-2596.

Cataloging-in-Publication Data
Names: Brundle, Harriet.
Title: Pollution / Harriet Brundle.
Description: New York : Gareth Stevens Publishing, 2022. | Series: InfoPics | Includes glossary and index.
Identifiers: ISBN 9781538270929 (pbk.) | ISBN 9781538270943 (library bound) | ISBN 9781538270936 (6 pack) | ISBN 9781538270950 (ebook)
Subjects: LCSH: Pollution--Juvenile literature.
Classification: LCC TD176.B747 2022 | DDC 363.73--dc23

Published in 2022 by
Gareth Stevens Publishing
29 East 21st Sreet
New York, NY 10010

© 2018 Booklife Publishing
This edition is published by arrangement with Booklife Publishing

Edited by: Emilie Dufresne
Designed by: Danielle Rippengill

All rights reserved. No part of this book may be reproduced in any form without permission in writing from the publisher, except by a reviewer.

Printed in the United States of America

CPSIA compliance Information: Batch #CW22GS: For further information contact Gareth Stevens, New York, New York at 1-800-542-2595.

Image Credits

Cover and throughout – Eky Studio, Maria Starus, LenaDushkina, Supriya07, billedfab, Tartila. 4&5 – Beresnev, nnnnae, Boyko.Pictures. 6&7 – Dzm1try, Finevector. 8&9 – Amanita Silvicora. 12&13 – piscari, supirloko89, avh_vectors. 14&15 – Dzianis_Rakhuba, Bakhtiar Zein, Maquiladora, Visual Generation, HappyPictures, Orakunya, SquishyDoom. 16&17 – Beresnev, avian. 18&19 – Alexandr III, Faber14, Raura7, Tartila. 20&21 – Sentavio, Visual Generation, miniwide, Biscotto Design, ViGor Art. 22&23 – Shany Muchnik, Colorcocktail, K-Nick, Usagi-P. All images courtesy of Shutterstock.com. With thanks to Getty Images, Thinkstock Photo and iStockphoto.

CONTENTS

Words that look like this can be found in the glossary on page 24.

ALL ABOUT POLLUTION

Pollution happens when materials, known as pollutants, are put into the environment.

These pollutants are harmful.

Earth is becoming more polluted every day.

Some forms of pollutants help to cause <u>global warming</u>, which is very bad for our planet.

We can all help to lower the amount of pollution on Earth.

AIR POLLUTION

When a harmful material is added to the air, it is called an air pollutant.

Pollutants enter the air from lots of different places.

There are over 1 billion cars in the world. Many cars burn fossil fuels to give them power.

Types of fossil fuels:

Oil

OIL

Gas

Coal

When fossil fuels are burned,
they cause air pollution.

Fossil fuels are used to
power lots of different
things, such as cars,
airplanes, and ships.

7

Air pollution can cause sneezing, coughing, itchy eyes, and more serious health problems.

Breathing in pollutants is bad for us. Millions of people around the world have had their health affected by air pollution.

Ninety percent of the people on Earth live in a place with poor air quality.

A lot of air pollution is caused by humans, but it can also be caused by natural events, such as a volcano erupting.

WATER POLLUTION

Water is polluted when harmful materials are added to it.

More than 70 percent of Earth is covered by water.

Animals can mistake plastic floating in the ocean for food and eat it. This can cause them harm.

Turtle

Jellyfish

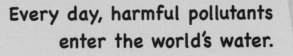

Every day, harmful pollutants enter the world's water.

HELP!

Around one truck full of plastic is
dumped into the ocean every minute.

Harmful pollutants can enter the world's water in many different ways.

HELP!

Ships leak oil into the ocean, which is harmful to plants and animals.

12

One of the ways pollutants are pumped into the ocean is through large pipes.

Ocean dumping is when pollutants are put straight into the ocean by humans on purpose. This could include garbage or <u>sewage</u>.

LAND POLLUTION

Every piece of trash, or garbage, you throw away must go somewhere.

Lots of garbage ends up in <u>landfills</u>. This causes land pollution.

Pollutants from the garbage in the landfill leak into the nearby soil. This can harm plant and animal life.

It is thought that millions of tons of waste are put into landfills around the world every year.

Pollutants from landfills may leak into nearby water.

Here are other ways our land can become polluted.

When lots of trees are cut down, the soil where the trees used to be can become badly damaged.

Some farmers use harmful sprays on their crops to stop animals and insects from eating them. These sprays pollute the soil, the air, and the nearby water.

Lots of the waste we throw away takes hundreds of years to break down.

Plastic bottles = around 450 years
Diapers = around 450 years
Plastic straws = around 200 years

LIGHT
POLLUTION

The overuse of man-made light causes light pollution.

Many night skies are lit by man-made light when they would naturally be dark. Light pollution is often worse in towns and cities.

Light pollution can be caused by things such as streetlights, homes, stadiums, billboards, and office buildings.

The **sky glow** from Los Angeles, California, can be seen from an airplane many miles away!

Light pollution can make it difficult for some people to sleep.

Light pollution can confuse animals.

NOISE POLLUTION

Noise pollution happens when too much unwanted noise is being made, often for long periods of time.

Noise pollution can be harmful to humans and animals.

Noise pollution can come from <u>construction</u>, trains, and airplanes.

Sounds above 85 <u>decibels</u> can harm your hearing.

A jet plane produces around 120–140 decibels and an electric drill produces around 95–100 decibels.

21

WHAT CAN WE DO?

Try to reduce how much garbage you throw away.

Reuse items when you can. For example, take reusable bags to the store instead of using plastic bags.

Use energy-saving light bulbs.

Turn off the lights when you leave the room.

PLASTIC

Walk or bike rather than using the car.

Recycle as much as possible. Glass, paper, and cans can all be recycled. Ask an adult to help you find out what other things you can recycle in your area.

GLOSSARY

construction	the act of building something
decibels	a unit used to measure loudness of a sound
environment	the natural world
fossil fuels	fuels, such as coal, oil, and gas, which formed millions of years ago from the remains of animals and plants
global warming	the slow rise of Earth's temperature
landfills	places where waste is buried
natural	found in nature and not made by people
quality	how good something is
recycle	to use again to make something else
sewage	wastewater from homes and factories that often includes human waste
sky glow	the brightness of the sky at night due to light pollution

INDEX